CW01034457

DEVON

WILDLIFE THROUGH THE SEASONS

John Walters

John Walters (signature)

Limited to 1000 copies

Leatherbound 1-50

Clothbound 51-1000

No.

© 2000 John Walters
Arlequin Press
26 Broomfield Road
Chelmsford
Essex CM1 1SW

www.arlequinpress.co.uk

Published 2000

ISBN 1 900159 51 1 Leatherbound
ISBN 1 900159 46 5 Clothbound

DEVON

WILDLIFE THROUGH THE SEASONS

John Walters

To my parents
Enid and Michael

Mute Swans on the Exeter Canal.

Goldfinches on teasels   Heathfield 20 January 2000

Goldfinches feeding on teasels.

1

Foreword

John is one of that dedicated band of painter/naturalists committed to watching in the wild and, whatever the difficulties, depicting the creature and something of its activity as it is happening.

In much the same way as prehistoric man the hunter relied on his skill, endurance and wiles in order to feed his kith and kin, today this drive resurfaces in those who enjoy the chase. Their ability to capture a vision of that which is often most difficult to find and record is severely tested. Certainly being out with John is to be shown the full gamut of fascination that exists within his patch, Devon. Over the years John has found a bewildering amount of its wildlife inhabitants and made it his business to get to know them. To accompany him is to learn that he is a quietly confident yet rather self-effacing guide, although ever present a glint in his eye betrays his underlying passion. These offerings to us are undoubtedly hard won.

In this book John shows the importance of the range of habitats each with its characteristic flora and fauna. It is satisfying to find Devon contains such a fund of rarities. Thirty-five years ago I began to tease out for myself an understanding of the habits of butterflies by watching and drawing them in the wild. Now nothing gives me greater satisfaction than to find members of the next generation utilising the same methods of outdoor field notation to help them achieve, develop and learn.

Of this select and yet ever growing band of dedicated artist/naturalists, learning from the wild, John is a perfect example of one who pushes the boundaries of what is possible ever further onwards.

These pages are vivid with the intensity of watching. John reveals through his drawings and commentary the behaviour of a living being, something which you find ever increasing in its interest. His results bring the involuntary gasp of admiration which has you wishing you'd been there with him. Often coming across wildlife in the most unlikely places and told with a wry humour; the range of wildlife that he conveys leaves me wondering at the span of his interest and knowledge.

The contents of this book are like a net of silver fish, John's catch of Devon wildlife as it is today is enspiriting and hopefully may engender in youngsters a desire to emulate. I hope the land of Devon will continue to be well-managed providing this wealth of interest in the future; for undoubtedly man's attempt to expand the boundaries of his attainment will ever remain.

David G. Measures March 2000

Acknowledgements

I would like to thank my parents for encouraging my early interest in wildlife and their continued support and enthusiasm. My brother, David, and sisters, Maria, Joanne, Nicola and Karen, for putting up with all the caterpillars, moths and beetles around the house as well as having a moth trap illuminating our garden!

My partner Joyce and sons Barnaby and Oscar for all their love, help and patience during the preparation of this book.

Dan Powell for encouraging my early attempts to sketch birds from life. James McCallum for providing me with so much inspiration over the last decade and for sharing his knowledge and enthusiasm for natural history and drawing.

To John Busby for his time, inspiration, and excellent advice on drawing and painting. David Measures for writing the foreword to this book. Also for his encouragement and advice, especially on handling watercolours, and for his company on memorable days spent painting butterflies in the field.

Jennie Hale for her company and shared enthusiasm whilst showing me the wildlife of her corner of Devon and Mike Langman for letting me have the prickly stick insect from his garden to sketch.

Norman Baldock of the Dartmoor National Park Authority for arranging for me to visit some of the secret corners of Dartmoor.

To Dean Hearn, Keith Stannard, Michael Brunning and their colleagues at Healeys Printers for their great care, expertise and skill in the printing of this book.

Lastly to Nigel Ede for inviting me to show my work in this form.

The edge of Dartmoor from Scoriton

3

Introduction

I have been a naturalist as far back as I can remember. Amongst my earliest memories are catching a slow worm and watching glow-worms in our garden on the South Downs in Hampshire.

When I was three my family moved to Hayling Island on the Hampshire coast and this is where I grew up. Although surrounded by superb bird filled harbours, it was insects that first captured my imagination. My interest in butterflies and moths began at infants school. Here I discovered the beautiful caterpillars of the lackey moth in a hedge by the playground. I remember on one occasion some of the caterpillars I had caught escaped in the classroom, much to the amusement of the other children.

At the age of eleven I began running a moth trap in my back garden. The variety of species caught was bewildering and a little confusing at first. This prompted me to start drawing them from life in an attempt to improve my identification skills. I was greatly encouraged by the late Eric Bradford of the Amateur Entomologists' Society when he praised my drawing attempts. For the next few years I concentrated on moths and their caterpillars, discovering much about their life cycles through observing, breeding and drawing them.

Although I took an interest in the birdlife of the area, it was not until my late teens that I took up birdwatching seriously. I naturally began drawing them but found the discipline of drawing moving subjects incredibly difficult. Looking back at

those early drawings and paintings they are stifled and lacking much life. A change in direction and inspiration came when I met a local wildlife artist Dan Powell. He was greatly influenced by the work of Eric Ennion, Lars Jonsson and John Busby. I was immediately attracted to this way of drawing wildlife subjects, capturing the natural liveliness and individual character of the subjects. I found this required great skill in both observation and drawing.

My early attempts to draw the movement of birds were desperately bad though I enjoyed doing them and took pleasure in the learning process, which would obviously be a long one.

I began studying at Falmouth School of Art in Cornwall in 1987. Whilst studying on a four year course in Graphic Design I had plenty of opportunities to get out sketching the wildlife of west Cornwall, especially on the Lizard Peninsular. This led to many memorable days in the field and I continued to learn more about the creatures I saw through drawing and painting them.

The most intensive spell of learning to draw wildlife came in my last year at Falmouth. I met up with James McCallum who had started a Fine Art Degree that year. We shared interests in wildlife and drawing and were at a similar stage in sketching them from life. Influenced by the work of Eric Ennion, John Busby, Lars Jonsson and David Measures we began to really try and work out what we were seeing and get it down on paper as accurately as we could. It was the start of a huge learning curve which we are both still on today. In the space of a few months we drew almost daily, expanding our studies to include the amazing rockpool life which we found in the area. None of the drawings were particularly good, to say the least, but each day a step forward, however small, was made.

After graduating we both attended John Busby's drawing course on the Firth of Forth. It was a great pleasure to meet John and David Measures and share their enthusiasm for wildlife and art. During the course much was learnt about drawing. Especially about the process of taking our sketches a step further and producing paintings which capture the whole scene of creatures interacting with each other and their environment. I left the course full of enthusiasm.

A few weeks later I moved to Devon to start working for the Dartmoor National Park Authority. I soon began to explore the estuaries, woods and moors of this beautiful county. Being such a large county it was difficult to get below the surface to start with. I purposely did not own a car at this time, preferring, as I still do today, to explore the countryside by bicycle.

Cycling, as well as keeping you fit, forces you to be out in all weathers, at all times of year. Whether cycling the twelve miles to work each day or being out on Dartmoor or the lanes of south Devon it is always a pleasure. Subtle changes in the hedgerows become much more noticeable and there are, of course, many more sightings of wildlife.

It took a few years before I really got to know the countryside and it began to reveal some of its secrets to me. Having the huge granite mass of Dartmoor close to the mild south coast of Devon makes it an area of contrasts. This mixture of northerly and southerly influences makes it a diverse and fascinating place for any naturalist.

Over time I have developed my own way of working. This involves concentrating on one area or species at a time (see Teign Estuary and Meadow Pipits). By doing this I continue to gain a deeper understanding of small pieces of the complex interactions between wildlife, landscape and the weather throughout the year.

I am equally happy visiting the coast on a special trip or just wandering around the local farmland and woods. I am also a keen gardener. My allotment, on a sunny hillside is a very productive area. It grows as many great green bush-crickets and other insects as it does vegetables!

Having subjects which can be watched within my daily routine and family life is essential to me. My interests in natural history are broad. Anything from tiny beetles and other insects to ravens and deer provide endless fascination. In a county like Devon there is always something new to be found. This may be the result of a particular search or by accident whilst looking for other species.

I now live with my partner Joyce and two young sons, Barnaby and Oscar, on the southern edge of Dartmoor. Working freelance enables me to concentrate on what I love doing. I now combine my drawing and painting with design work and ecological studies.

Buckfastleigh, March 2000

Spring

Spring comes early to the Devon countryside and is the most fickle of all the seasons. A mild spell in February can bring a rush of activity: early spring flowers; a marked increase in birdsong; and even a few butterflies tempted out of hibernation. Just when the end of winter seems close, hopes are dashed by the return to icy weather. This feels twice as cold as it really is.

These cold snaps rarely last long and during milder interludes, the pace of life quickens. Spring flowers are the most welcome sign of things to come. By the end of February the main flush of snowdrops along the hedgebanks begins to fade away as the sunny yellow celandines replace them. There are few more welcome sights than of these waxy flowers, standing bright and resilient on a sunny morning after a period of bad weather. Within a few weeks they are joined by the main flush of primroses, wood anemones or windflowers, dog violets,

Celandines

wild daffodils, ramsons and bluebells. The Devon hedgebanks are now at their very best, enlivened by small tortoiseshell butterflies and queen bumblebees fresh from hibernation. On the first warm days the bumblebees are joined by other early insects. They gather on the yellow sallow catkins for the first feast of the year. Not surprisingly it is in these bushes that the first migrant birds, chiffchaffs, can be observed busily searching for a meal.

Other creatures are stirring from hibernation too. On mild, damp evenings frogs and toads are often seen crossing roads as they return to their breeding ponds and ditches. Even though they squirm and wriggle strongly in my grasp, I always give a helping hand to any I find.

Common Toad

Spells of warmer weather dramatically increase bird activity. By April blackbirds are singing strongly at dawn and dusk, whilst overhead the buzzards are revelling in the first thermals and spiralling up in noisy groups as pairs sort out their breeding territories. In the woods the repetitive calls of great and marsh tits fill the air. Blue tits perform their gliding song flights amongst the trees in between spells of searching out likely looking nest holes. Whilst mistle thrushes are already on eggs, woodpeckers drum out their territories. In a few woods the elusive lesser spotted

Buzzards

Common Lizard

lizards fresh from hibernation. These first warm days are the best time to look for these shy creatures. They can be approached closely as they are intent on absorbing all the warmth they can in readiness for another summer of activity.

woodpecker can now be seen drumming and displaying. Activity amongst these resident birds is at a peak on these first warm sunny mornings of the year.

On moors and heaths the first fine days incite the skylarks and meadow pipits into song. This activity is usually brought to an abrupt halt as the wind turns to the north again bringing hail and snow showers and a return to winter. At this time of year the beautiful low whistles of golden plovers can still be heard as the flocks wheel nervously overhead seeking a quiet place to continue feeding. The Scottish and Icelandic spring is still a long way off for these northern birds.

If you seek out sunny spots, sheltered from any cold northerly winds, you may happen upon basking adders and common

On still days the songs of newly arrived wheatears and ring ouzels can be heard. The "tick-tocking" of snipe and wild "koor-li" of curlews echo over the bogs and mires. Stonechats have begun nesting amongst the heather and gorse.

The cold edge to the weather is usually lost by early May. This is the month of greatest change, often so rapid as to make it difficult to keep up with the pace of activity. Winter views are quickly lost in the expanding canopy and the hedgebanks flush with growth. By mid-May the early spring flowers are fading to seed, lost amongst the vegetation. Stitchwort, red campion and hedge mustard, among others, now replace them. Male orange-tip butterflies provide a splash of colour and activity to the hedgerows. As evening approaches they can often be found resting close to the lady's smock and garlic mustard flower heads. Their beautiful dappled-green underwings provide excellent camouflage amongst these flowers.

Bird migration is now at a peak, especially on the coast. The wintering waders and wildfowl depart and migrant terns, skuas and divers, as well as land birds, arrive. Each week brings fresh arrivals: willow warblers singing sweetly in woodland clearings; blackcaps and the occasional garden warbler in thicker patches of scrub; and the excited chattering songs of swallows gradually filling their territories in farmyards and town gardens. When a high screaming call is heard on a warm May morning, you know that summer is almost upon us. The sound of parties of swifts chasing each other over the rooftops is a welcome sound, evocative of a balmy summer evening after a blisteringly hot day.

As these migrants arrive the resident species already have fledged young. Blackbirds, song thrushes and robins can be seen gathering food everywhere. Walking along a riverbank an excited call draws attention to a young dipper suddenly bursting into life as its parent appears with food.

May is a month of lush fresh green leaves. To my eyes, these appear best in overcast damp weather when the lush variety of greens really stand out against the leaden sky.

The resident woodland birds have now been joined by other summer visitors. Pied flycatchers are difficult to see but their

Wood Warbler

Orange-tip roosting

short and simple song rings out in upland oak woods. Wood warblers dash around amongst the delicate fresh oak and beech leaves singing their trilling song almost continuously.

They seem the most exicited of all the returning migrants singing with so much gusto that they literally shake as they finish their trills.

By the end of May the scene is set for summer. The first really warm days subtly change the pace of life in the countryside. As fresh greens darken, and the main flush of growth in the hedgebanks fades there is a sense that the pace of life, although still hectic, has slowed a fraction. The first wild strawberries can now be picked along the hedgebanks, a real taste of summer.

Wood Anemone or Windflower

Primroses

Dippers

Amongst the crashing white water of a Dartmoor river sits a dipper. It has the appearance of an overgrown wren, earth brown, with a dapper white bib and chestnut belly. Suddenly it launches itself into the water and disappears below, only to bob to the surface a few moments later with a caddis fly case in its bill. After swimming to the nearest boulder it bashes the case to extract the juicy larva, has a quick preen, blinks a few times, then launches itself into the water once more. These amazing birds really are at one with the torrent rivers and streams they inhabit.

It is a privilege to live with these birds virtually on my doorstep. Three tributaries join the River Dart near my home as the rivers descends from the high ground of Dartmoor. This is perfect dipper country. The clean moorland rivers are ideally suited to the species and here they seem to be at saturation level with at least ten pairs breeding within a few miles of my home.

Being resident birds they can be observed at any time of year but are at their best from just after the new year through to early spring. Activity is at a peak during periods when the river levels are low. At this time there is great excitement as pair bonds are being established and territories defended. This involves a lot of singing and some amazing displays. I have found that the best time to watch these displays is just after dawn. The dippers leave their

winter roost sites under bridges and in old buildings around the town and head out to their daytime territories.

A good forecast sees me up before dawn, which fortunately isn't too difficult in January and February! Leaving the house in the cold still air a dipper's call can be heard. The bird is seen silhouetted against the pale blue sky as it flies, wavering erratically from side to side, over the rooftops. It drops down to the river further on and it is here that I see it again.

Approaching cautiously I conceal myself by the side of a bridge. The dipper is singing just below me. At first only its white bib can be seen in the dim light, then as daylight gradually increases, its plump form can be made out. Suddenly another excited call is heard and a second bird appears from nowhere on the same shingle bank. This excites the first bird into full display mode with its shivering wings held out and its head held up to the other bird, displaying its white throat and bib to the full. This displaying is accompanied by loud singing and lasts for some time but there is no aggression between the birds, it is the greeting display of an already established pair. Sometimes the pair will fly up and sit on the wall by the bridge only to be disturbed by passing pedestrians and cars as people make their way to work.

It is only in spring that I have seen dippers well away from the

Trespassing dippers will quickly be chased off amidst much singing and displaying. To avoid any confrontation dippers leaving their roost sites further upstream overfly this pair's territory calling loudly.

Where pairs do meet on the edge of territories I have seen them displaying head to head singing furiously with their heads held high and bills almost touching.

immediate vicinity of a river or stream. Often whilst cycling around the lanes the hard "spitch" call will be heard, often difficult to place at first being out of its usual context. The calling dipper is then seen high in the sky as it flies from one river system to another. After hearing a commotion on the river below my allotment one sunny March afternoon, a pair of dippers flew up. They climbed high into the sky until they were just dots in the blue before heading off east, probably towards the tributaries of the river Teign. These must have been a newly established pair seeking out a breeding territory in this already overcrowded area.

As their habitat is very rarely affected by freezing conditions dippers generally breed early. The earliest pairs being those which use traditional nest sites. These are often on bridges where the large dome-shaped nests have become part of the bridge itself and just need patching up and re-lining before they are ready to use. One pair I have watched over several years usually has young fledged around the middle of April when other pairs are just finishing lining their nests. New nests take some time to build so the pair can be observed at length as they collect sticks and moss to build the structure. Along one stretch of the River Dart I have often observed pairs collecting dead beech leaves with which to line their nests.

I have only managed to observe the courtship and mating of a pair of dippers once. This was on a warm evening in early April. The pair were extremely excited closely chasing each other in wild flights over the river. Whenever they landed on a boulder there was much exaggerated displaying and singing with heads held high and their tails fully fanned out. Eventually the female adopted a submissive pose with wings

Dippers gathering moss and beech leaves to line thier nest

12

shivering and the male mounted her briefly with his wings still whirring.

Activity around the nest site goes quiet whilst the eggs are being incubated and it is often difficult to find the birds at all. This changes once the young hatch. This is the busiest time of the year for any bird, and the pair hurry backwards and forwards carrying the larvae of various aquatic insects and the occasional small fish to the young. Just before fledging the grey heads of the young huddle in the nest entrance showing their huge orange gapes and calling loudly whenever an adult comes in view. Once I was lucky enough to visit a nest just as the young had fledged. The three youngsters sat huddled on a floating log in the river bobbing up and down in unison – an amusing sight to watch. Within a day the young have stationed themselves along the river. These locations are surprisingly similar from year to year. One is a little way downstream and the other quite a way upstream. Here the young birds sit like stones tight in against the river bank and are easily missed as you walk past. The appearance of an adult brings them to life again with gape open and wings quivering.

I have often observed the adults singing to the juvenile even whilst feeding it. I presume it is teaching the youngster how to sing as this is an important aspect of the lives of all dippers, who sing to defend winter and breeding territories.

During high summer, as with the rivers and streams to which they are so intimately attached, dipper activity is at a low ebb. Those that are seen are usually rather tatty looking individuals in heavy moult sitting quietly on riverside boulders.

Cooler autumn conditions with a fresh flow in the rivers sees them back on form as they sing to set up winter feeding territories. These are defended throughout the winter except when the rivers are in flood. At these times the dippers retreat up the side streams and are often to be found on tiny streamlets in farmland, well away from the main river. Then, when the river levels drop again they move back, take up territories and begin the yearly cycle again.

Dipper adult singing to recently fledged juvenile.

13

Adult Dipper feeding newly fledged juvenile.

Adult Dipper feeding newly fledged young straight from the water. The young were fed a variety of aquatic invertebrates and the occasional small fish.

In search of the Blue Ground Beetle

During the early 1980s it was thought that the Blue Ground Beetle had disappeared from its last known haunts in Devon and Cornwall. Sightings had been few and far between in the ancient woodlands where it had once occurred. Then two isolated populations were found surviving on the southern edge of Dartmoor in woodlands where the beetle had last been recorded by Victorian entomologists. Although proved to be still resident the beetle was still regarded as a species vulnerable to extinction in this country, and globally threatened.

There was just a chance that other colonies existed, and early in 1996 I became involved in conducting searches for it around Dartmoor. This was quite a challenge considering the number of woodlands which had potential for holding this elusive beast. The following is an account of my first day searching and some incredible beginner's luck.

The 24 April 1996 was a day of sunshine and showers. Spring had been slow coming and it was only then that the primroses, violets and celandines were showing in force. I was to spend the day in a wooded valley close to my home. After an early start I set off on my bike towards the moor. The first part of this journey was the steepest, climbing up through some woodland. As I steadily ascended, a lesser spotted woodpecker's 'kee-kee-kee' call rang out from amidst the trees. I stopped to

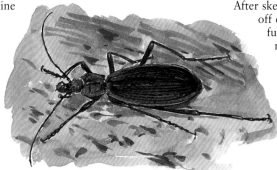

Blue Ground Beetle

catch my breath and look for it amongst the oak branches. But, as is so often the case, I could not catch a glimpse of it. Towards the top of the hill signs of the warmer weather included a huge oil beetle and a strange-looking segmented larva crossing the road. The latter was a glow-worm larva, the first of many I would see during the spring and early summer.

After a quick descent into the river valley I crossed the river by the old packhorse bridge and locked up my bike in the car park. As I set off my first wood warbler of the year sang from high up in an oak, but it was moving about too quickly to enable me to get a good view. Insect activity, held back by the cold conditions, had suddenly burst into life. Reaching a sandy area by the river there were hundreds of tiny bees each busy cleaning out its burrow. I watched them for a while as their activity waxed and waned with the passing shower clouds.

After sketching them for a short while I set off on a long walk which would take me further upstream towards the open moor. After a while I entered a strange wood. Its steep sided floor was littered with boulders and dead wood and these were covered in a mossy green carpet. The wood had once been a working coppice but had been abandoned for the past sixty years allowing the coppice stools of the oak to regrow. Now it was left to the sheep and ponies which wander in from the moorland to find shelter and food, a perfect ancient pasture woodland. The path ran out and I had to pick my way carefully down to the river to make any headway. I turned over a few pieces of wood and rocks on my way but where do you start looking for beetles in a place that is made for them to hide in?

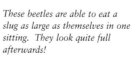

Further upstream I reached a rocky riverside platform and stopped for some lunch. A hard 'spitch' call preceded the whirring form of a dipper as it flew downstream over the white water before settling on a boulder. I idly watched it whilst eating my sandwiches then noticed several large pondskaters in some shallow pools beside me. With them was a smaller species which I had not come across before. I quickly sketched it and later identified it as a water cricket, '*a species which favours shady woodland pools*'. My planned route would then take me up onto the moorland well above the river. So after continuing upstream for a short distance I started the sharp ascent. The going was slow, scrambling over the huge moss covered boulders, and I lost my footing a couple of times as the moss carpet gave way beneath my feet.

Water Cricket

By mid-afternoon I was half way up the slope. I noticed a dead oak, with peeling bark ahead of me. Remembering that this was the sort of place that the beetle had been found in the past I stopped to investigate. As I carefully lifted the first piece of bark an *Abax* beetle scurried into the shadows away from the light. Then, peering under an adjacent piece I could just make

out the silhouette of a much larger beetle with long spidery legs. "It can't be" I thought, whilst slowly peeling back the bark. As the strong afternoon sun struck the beetle, it lit up as a glistening, blue-black jewel reflecting a deep cobalt as well as greens and purples. The colours reminded me of those that can be seen in oil patches on wet roads. The very first tree and it was in the bag. I stood stunned not believing my luck. Little was I to know that this would be the first of many.

Time was getting on so I continued up through the wood, stopping to turn over a few other pieces of dead bark. It was not long before another of these huge beetles fell out amongst a shower of earth, shavings and woodlice. It was getting too easy! I left the wood and climbed up above the gorge. From here there were superb views of the sunlit woodland across the valley. More shower clouds came over as I worked my way back to my bike and set off on the steep climb out of the valley.

Since that occasion I have spent many hours studying this fascinating beetle in an attempt to find out more about its ecology and why it is so rare. Being nocturnal it is best searched for on damp spring nights, when the adult beetles climb the moss covered oak trunks to search for their favourite prey – slugs.

These beetles are able to eat a slug as large as themselves in one sitting. They look quite full afterwards!

Lesser Spotted Woodpeckers

Once learnt, the distinctive "kee-kee-kee" call is the best indication of the presence of one of these tiny woodpeckers. Even then it often takes a while before the bird is seen, usually high in the branches of a tree. The drumming is subtly different to its larger relative, quieter and more prolonged against the short explosive blast of a greater spotted. A good way to tell them apart is to time the drum. A lesser spotted's last for about one and a half seconds whilst that of the greater spotted is difficult to time at all, lasting about half a second. The lesser spotted is also more likely to repeat its drum several times with short intervals.

I had read about this species' spring displays when the pair would perform 'butterfly' flights and it became an ambition to observe and sketch these displays. It would take four springs of intense observation before this ambition was fully realised.

The first step came in the form of occasional winter sightings in a local wood. The birds were present in what looked to me like good breeding habitat. Spring visits in 1993 led to occasional sightings but no display flights. It was not until 20 March 1994 that my luck changed.

The frost was just beginning to thaw as I walked slowly up through the woods. Approaching a clearing the drumming of a woodpecker could be heard and, thinking it was a greater spotted, I wandered over to have a look. To my surprise it was a red-capped male lesser spotted on a splintered oak branch. As I stood in the bright sunlight, a second bird joined him. The male began to tap very slowly, then ran up a branch with his wings held up, then flew following the second bird into the wood.

Although very brief I had glimpsed the 'butterfly' flight and was eager to see more. Twenty minutes later the male was back drumming on the same branch and again flew off, in butterfly fashion, to the same area of woodland. I later searched in vain for him there. Over the next few weeks I saw and heard several drumming birds but saw no more display.

It was not until the following spring that I began watching these birds again. With the birth of a son, Barnaby, time for idly wandering around the woods was suddenly very restricted. The answer to this was to take him out with me in a sling for an early morning walk, whilst his mum had a well-deserved lie-in. He would be asleep within minutes of leaving the house and usually remain so for at least a couple of hours, allowing me plenty of time to wander around the woods. Being unable to carry my full sketching kit I was reduced to the bare essentials of binoculars, A5 sketchpad and a felt-tip pen.

The first sightings came in late February, a female which frequented a small area of oaks. One morning the 'kee-kee' calls she was making were different, being slightly slower than usual. When I eventually caught sight of her she was displaying, often immediately after a short flight between branches. I was able to watch and sketch this activity for about half an hour. At one point she landed on the underside of a small branch and displayed in a manner which reminded me of a bird of paradise. I found her displaying in the same area a couple of weeks later but she appeared to be alone. Even though I located three other sites in the wood where there were drumming birds, no more display or signs of nesting activity were seen, although surely this was taking place. They went quiet in early May, presumably as nesting commenced. This, coupled with

Displaying Lesser Spotted Woodpeckers.

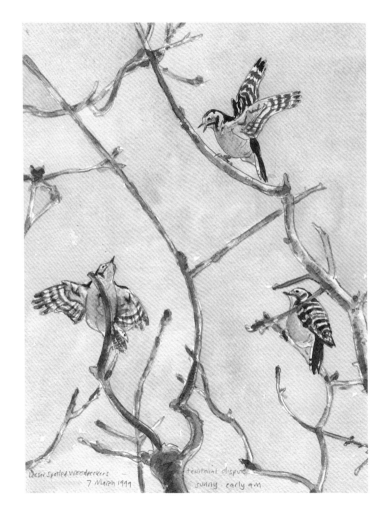

19

the unfolding canopy, made observations difficult and I would have to wait for another season before seeing them again.

Experience gained over the previous seasons paid off in 1996. Barnaby now accompanied me in a backpack and I also had time to visit on my own, taking my telescope and painting kit. The familiar 'kee-kee-kee' call rang out from the oaks one day in mid-January and I found two birds that day. Despite regular visits they proved very elusive and it was not until mid-March that I had any further sightings. It was a male I finally caught up with, his calls betraying his presence high in an oak. He was actively searching for food, often shuffling backwards in a spiral down a branch. With sewing-machine like pecks he sounded out the wood for the borings of beetle larvae.

Woodpecker activity really took off at the end of March during a settled spell of weather with early morning frosts. Following the sound of a drumming bird, I glimpsed a pair twisting and turning as they flipped past me from a clearing into the wood. This was the area in which I had first seen the display, so an early start was called for the next day.

A thick frost lay on the ground as I cycled up to the wood. After locking up my bike I began walking slowly through the wood carefully checking the tree tops for woodpeckers. A few blue tits glided in display flights here but little else stirred in the cold morning air. Then, as the sun cleared the hills to the south, bird activity increased dramatically. Reaching the area where I had seen them the previous day I set up my telescope to view a likely looking tree. My luck was in. Within seconds a female flew in and started drumming. She then flew low over me and drummed on a dead branch above

my head. The sun was now beginning to light up the clearing and warm the treetops. Another bird called on the far side of the clearing and the female immediately flew over towards it. The second bird was a male. The pair then joined together in some energetic displays which involved wing raising and butterfly flights as they chased each other around the bare branches. Suddenly a second male flew in inciting some wild displays from the pair.

A chase ensued with the birds adopting an exaggerated 'hoopoe-like' butterfly flight accompanied by loud 'kee-kee-kee' calls. One of them interpersed its butterfly flight with brief glides, the wings being held up in a V, which reminded me of a nightjar's glide. The activity was frantic. I only had time to watch them in amazement for a minute or so before all three flew into the edge of the wood. I lost sight of the female at this time but continued to watch the males as they tried to outdrum each other. They were in oak trees 30 metres apart and drummed alternately for about a quarter of an hour. Then only one bird seemed to remain. It carried on drumming, as well as feeding and calling, in an old oak for the next hour until it too disappeared into the wood.

My ambition was now truly satisfied, the knowledge gained from three years of observation had really paid off. Getting up early and being on site as the first rays of sun warm the treetops was the key to seeing these amazing displays. Throughout the rest of that spring I spent many hours observing and sketching the displaying birds until they were hidden amongst the leaves by early June. All my attempts to locate nest holes ended in vain. Watching that part of their lives will have to wait for another season.

♀ drumming - rival ♀ flew
in and chased her from
perch - then a lot of
calling & wing displays

v. close views right above
my head - birds seem oblivious
of ground predators - maybe because
they (never?) feed on the ground

21

Colston Road, Buckfastleigh
21 March 1999 pm

Rooks at their nest on a windy April afternoon.

22

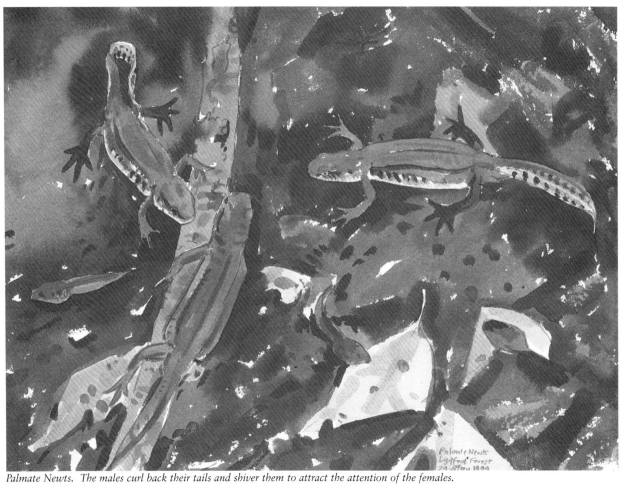

Palmate Newts. The males curl back their tails and shiver them to attract the attention of the females.

23

I was drawn by some very strange calls coming from the edge of the woods one mild March morning. At first it sounded like a dove, then a creaky gate before ending with some hard stuttering calls. Thinking it may be some woodpeckers I moved closer and found a small group of jays.

There were at least four present in the oaks, moving about slowly in the undergrowth and hopping into the tree tops with their crests raised high and rump feathers puffed up. One bird appeared with a clump of lichen in its bill and sat staring at the others for a minute or so. I could only presume that it was some sort of territorial dispute.

Sensing my presence they slowly disappeared amongst the oaks leaving me to ponder over their strange behaviour.

Jays - territorial dispute? 2 pairs involved - one flew in with lichen in bill others displaying with rumps & crest feathers raised - creaky gate and clever tree calls 2-25am overcast calm mild 17 March 1996

24

Great Green Bush-cricket & Common Groundhopper adult
nymph
on Marigold flower Allotment Boothstown   26 May 1999

Adult Common Groundhopper and newly hatched Great Green
Bush-cricket nymph sunning themselves on a marigold flower.

Emperor Moth

During the extremely hot weather of August 1995 I set about the task of finding an emperor moth caterpillar to illustrate for an identification guide I was working on. As this is a fairly common species on Dartmoor I imagined it would be a relatively easy task. This was not to be the case.

16 August 1995 I started my search on a very hot afternoon at Bovey Heath. After an hour I gave up as I would be visiting a site on Dartmoor, where I had previously found them, the next day.

17 August 1995 Parking my bike by a farm, I set off up the rough track which leads to the open moor. As I passed through the moor gate and set off up the slope I was soon into an area of flowering heather. Small Tortoiseshell butterflies, well away from their nettle patches, were out on the moor feeding on the heather flowers. Swallows from the local farms were also taking advantage of the warm still conditions and hawking over the moorland. After a couple of hours, with the conditions getting much warmer, I gave up searching amongst the heather and bilberry gullies having had no success. Had they fed up early in the warm weather and already pupated?

18 August 1995 One last attempt. As I cycled up to Haytor Down in heatwave conditions sweat poured off my forehead stinging my eyes. Another search around some disused quarries for an hour or so produced some old Emperor moth egg cases. I was getting closer!

Further along the road the yellow of the western gorse complemented the bell heather and ling beautifully in the late afternoon sunshine. I decided to make one last search around Saddle Tor where I had seen adult emperor moths flying around in previous years. Still no luck and time and patience seemed to be running out. I finally admitted defeat and set off for home. As I cycled past Blackslade Mire I was thinking 'I bet one walks across the road in front of me now' when there it was! A fat, green, spotted caterpillar racing across the tarmac in front of my wheel. I could hardly believe what I was seeing. On reaching home I set about sketching it, as by morning it would be spun up in a thick cocoon.

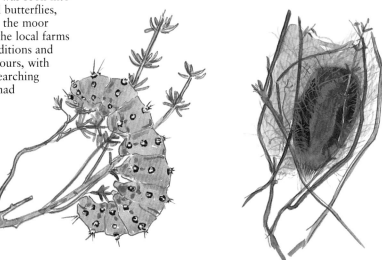

The cocoon remained in an old yoghurt pot by the back door throughout the winter months. Then arriving home one May evening a large female moth was sitting on the cocoon.

In these first moments when the colours are pristine, the wings are like deep velvet. They do not remain so for long and it is a privilege to witness this fleeting first stage.

I was keen to see how well this species' renowned scent attraction would work. Especially after reading accounts of a male picking up a female's scent from over a mile away, and records of over eighty males being attracted to one virgin female!

The following afternoon was warm and sunny as I cycled steadily upwards towards Haytor. Having reached the highest point of my journey I began to freewheel down towards Saddle Tor. I soon saw a male emperor moth flying acrosss the road in front of me. He seemed to be working in lines across the heather, presumably searching for the scent of a virgin female.

I got off my bike, then, after getting out my sketchpad, put the female moth down onto some gorse and waited. The speed of the males' reaction shocked me. Within seconds one had flown in and immediately mated. I could see the reason for his haste and lack of courtship as seconds later more males appeared from nowhere over the heather. These late comers had just missed their chance but still settled on the female. At one point there were three other males fluttering around the mating pair. All these moths attracted the attentions of the local stonechats and at least one of the unlucky suitors made a welcome addition to their broods' diet.

15 May 1996 *warm, sunny afternoon*

3.00pm - *put female moth onto gorse by road*
near Saddle Tor

3.01pm - *a male immediately flew in and mated with her*

3.02pm - *then 5 or 6 other males came hurtling in from the*
surrounding moorland. Some crash land near the female.

3.07pm - *the female has lost her attraction to the passing males.*

3.25pm - *the pair parted, and the male flew off.*

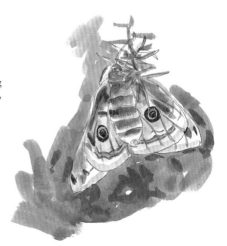

I released her further along the road at Coldeast Cross, close to where the caterpillar had originally been found. The now empty yoghurt pot obviously still contained some scent. A male came buzzing around me for a minute or so afterwards, before losing interest and heading out across the moorland.

Goosanders

Goosanders are true river ducks, at their best amongst the crashing white water of a torrent river. Their breeding range has been slowly expanding southwards this century and during the past decade they have become established on the Dartmoor rivers.

Breeding activity starts early in the year as the males begin to display in small groups to the females. These displays involve skimming over the surface with their head feathers puffed out, rising up out of the water and occasionally shooting their neck and head forward, stiffening for a second before relaxing again.

The females either chatter back harshly with their punk crests raised or continue resting or preening, pretending to ignore the posturing of the males.

River Dart Dartbridge 21 Feb 1999

Goosanders displaying.

Long-tailed Tits

For two years in a row I watched this species nest building in the bare branches of oaks in my local woods. They tirelessly collected lichen, moss and feathers for their beautiful nest. But I was not the only one watching – on both occasions I returned a few days later to find the nest in tatters on the ground. The local carrion crows were prime suspects but it may have been a jay.

Despite these setbacks long-tailed tits do breed successfully in this area. The nests which fledge the most young are always those built in the safety of a gorse bush.

Longtailed Tits Hembury Woods 20 March 1995

A Pied Flycatcher sitting quietly on branch - suddenly startled by wood ants
Yarner Wood 28 April 1994

Pied flycatcher disturbed by wood ants.

Bee-flies and oil beetles

These insects are amongst the first to appear on warm spring mornings. Although not closely related they share similar, if somewhat bizzare, life cycles. Bee-flies are often seen nectaring on celandines and other early flowers. On close examination they are truly exceptional insects, with boldly patterned wings, large eyes and a long proboscis – like something out of science fiction!

Bee-fly

The oil beetles (named after their habit of exuding oil from their bodies and leg joints if picked up) can be found in a variety of situations from coastal footpaths to meadows and woodlands. There are two common species which are very similar in appearance. They are usually seen moving rapidly across a path in a rather gangling manner, or feeding on leaves and petals – celandine flowers are a favourite.

Mating pair of oil beetles

Both insects are parasites of small bees and lay eggs in the soil near their nests. They are unusual amongst insects in having an extra stage in their development, a pre-larva. Oil beetle females lay thousands of eggs in small pits at the edges of paths. The tiny pre-larvae climb up onto flower heads and attach themselves to any hairy insect which visits the flower. The tiny fraction that survive are those lucky enough to attach themselves to the right species of bee - no wonder they have to lay so many eggs.

Adders

Whilst walking across moors and heaths searching for snakes I find my senses are sharpened considerably. Anything remotely snakelike causes me to stop dead in my tracks. Often all that I have seen is a twisted stem of gorse but every now and then I am rewarded with views of an adder.

Early in the spring they are usually coiled tightly in the cold air. But on warmer days they stretch out, often draping themselves over the low gorse and heather. If approached carefully it is possible to get excellent views as the snake stares back with its golden-flecked red eyes.

first Adder of the year - Bovey Heath 21 February 2000
cold wind but sunny and warm in sheltered spots several common Lizards

Narrow-bordered Bee Hawks

It is always a treat to watch these day flying moths which look and behave more like high-speed bumblebees. There are two British species named after the broad or narrow borders to their otherwise clear wings. The narrow-bordered is the larger of the two and closely resembles a carder bee. It inhabits meadows and woodland rides where an abundance of devil's-bit scabious, the larva's foodplant, grows.

On Dartmoor they are mainly found in the wet meadows known as rhôs pastures. These areas are traditionally managed by the hill farmers of Dartmoor and have never been ploughed or subjected to herbicides. They are grazed only during late summer and autumn with South Devon cattle.

A buff-coloured blur moving too fast to register properly was my first encounter with a bee hawk. It flew like a super-charged bumblebee with amazing swiftness around a meadow. It seemed almost impossible to watch let alone sketch. But with experience and patience it was possible to observe the moths nectaring at close range. I soon learned that the flowers of bird's-foot trefoil and lousewort are their favourites.

Although found in scattered sites around Dartmoor bee hawks usually occur in low densities over a wide area. This particular small meadow is a special site for them as here they are quite common.

To obtain good views of a bee hawk requires patience or speed. You must either wait by a nectar source until one arrives to feed, or attempt to follow individuals in flight until they appear to stop in an area, then run towards the spot and hope to find them feeding. I found the latter method was most successful.

Whilst feeding, their wings remain beating so fast as to appear almost invisible. Only occasionally when probing the deep flowers of lousewort do they momentarily stop, allowing the clear wings with dark borders and veins to be seen.

They are most active during mid-morning and again during late afternoon, often becoming quite torpid during the heat of midday. One individual I was watching flew into an alder bordering the meadow and sat sunning on a leaf for a minute or so before almost falling to the ground and settling in the low grasses. Here it was possible to pick it up.

Occasionally whilst following a bee hawk it repeatedly settles in areas where there are clearly no flowers. These are egg laying females which fly low, occasionally settling briefly to 'test' the vegetation with their legs. If they detect a scabious plant the abdomen is curled onto the nearest piece of vegetation and a green pearl-like egg laid. This is not always onto the foodplant, often being laid on a nearby grass stem. The abundance of the foodplant in the meadow would ensure that the newly hatched larva will not have to wander far for a meal.

A small spider with a lot of nerve was the only predator I have ever seen attempting to catch a bee hawk - it was soon shaken off!

Returning to the meadow in late July and August is always a surprise. After a few brief weeks the vegetation becomes quite lush.

At this time the larvae of the bee hawks are quite easy to find. It is just a matter of looking for scabious plants which have been nibbled then searching amongst the leaves. The spike-tailed larvae come in two forms. Either plain green or green marked with purple-red lines along the sides and back, and always with purple on the underside which perfectly matches the colour of the scabious stems.

A few which I took home to rear pupated in a loose cocoon amongst surface litter, and I imagine that they do so in similar situations in the wild. The resultant moths are something of a surprise as, when freshly emerged, the wings are not transparent but covered in a bloom of dusty grey scales. This condition does not last for long as the scales are lost during the very first flight. My greatest pleasure in rearing one of these moths is to take it back to the spot where the caterpillar was found. It prepares for flight on your fingertip before whirring off into the meadow. I can follow it for a few moments before it is lost to view.

Bee hawks nectaring on bluebells. At other flowers they would feed for a few seconds at a time but here they would often remain at one nectar source for up to half a minute allowing superb close views. As they moved amongst the flowers their yellow, pollen covered tongues, were kept semi-coiled ready to be probed deeply upwards into the flowers as they hovered almost vertically below.

Newly arrived Sand Martins inspecting a nest hole.

House Martins collecting dried grass stems with which to line their nests.

Jackdaws

Although roguish in appearance I find the activities of these small crows to be highly amusing, endearing and full of character. Unlike many birds they form long pair bonds which are maintained through mutual preening. They are an opportunist species, at home in a variety of situations from sea cliffs to town centres, often taking advantage of the activities of people for food and shelter.

Near my home the local jackdaw population can be split into two groups: those that nest in a disused quarry from which most of the birds head out to feed in the surrounding farmland; and other individuals which spend most of their time in the town, nesting under rooftops and feeding on scraps. Their sharp eyes are always quick to take advantage of opportunities as they watch from their lookout posts. Discarded scraps or crumbs are quickly scraped from the pavement with a sideways action of the head before they flip back to the rooftops and safety. Their diet seems to consist of anything they can find, ranging from kitchen scraps to drowsy butterflies and other insects caught in aerial sallies.

Spring is a time of noisy activity as pairs collect sticks to build their rather untidy nests. These are usually tucked away under rooftops though some birds nest in

chimneys often annoying the residents by depositing large numbers of twigs, and sometimes themselves, into the fireplace! A few pairs breed under a bridge carrying a busy main road. Here their nests are constantly shaken by the noise and vibration of the traffic inches above their heads but they don't seem to mind.

After the young have fledged, the quarry nesting birds spend most of their time out in the fields. Here they often consort with large flocks of carrion crows and rooks, only returning to the quarry occasionally during the day and at night to roost.

Jackdaw getting to grips with some nesting material.

In very windy weather Jackdaws revel in the up-draughts against the rock faces of the quarry as they tumble and dive in noisy groups.

Jackdaws feeding on scraps left by visitors to Buckfast Abbey.

Summer

The momentum of spring activity in the countryside continues well into early summer. Bird song often lulls in early June when the nesting season is in full swing, but there is a noticeable rise in volume by mid-month as many pairs prepare to raise a second brood. The dawn chorus, still strong throughout June gradually dies away in the first weeks of July. Foxgloves are now a prominent feature along the hedgebanks and in woodlands. They provide a visible clock which counts down to high summer. The flowers begin at the base of the spikes in early June gradually moving up the stem through the month. They have all gone to seed by late July.

Insect and plant activity reaches a peak with the long days and warmer weather. Lush meadows are thick with green as the grasses flower, sending clouds of pollen into the air. Then the buzz of insects and chirrups of grasshoppers increase in volume as the grasses gradually go to seed and turn to brown.

Foxgloves

Not all birds are quiet. In high summer the songs of yellowhammers, whitethroats and woodpigeons seem to rise in volume on hot summer afternoons. The woodpigeon's lazy drawn out calls, seem to become even more sleepy, a sound evocative of a hot and hazy summer afternoon.

In the woodlands the clamour of tit flocks fills the trees. The birds themselves are usually just glimpsed as they feed up in the thick canopy which has now matured to a deep shade of green. The majority of these birds are youngsters, soft yellow versions of the adults. In certain localities on warm calm days an audible rustle can be heard from the woodland floor. It is the noise of thousands of industrious wood ants as they hurry about collecting nest material and food amongst last year's dead leaves.

Orange-tip caterpillar

The hedgebanks have also turned a darker shade of green as the main flowering period is over. Exceptions are the pale pink blossoms of brambles and the dense flowerheads of marjoram. These attract a host of bees, gatekeeper butterflies and other insects. The orange-tip butterflies have now gone but look closer at the seedpods of the hedge mustard and you may find their excellently camouflaged caterpillars.

Gorse seed pods crackle in the afternoon heat on moorland slopes as the last pipit and skylark songs trail away. The sharp calls of young wheatears can be heard around quarries, tors and stone walls. Nearby moorland bogs abound with insects. Especially noticeable are the beautiful keeled skimmer dragonflies tussling with each other low over the sphagnum carpet. Other insects are not quite so welcome for any observers – the biting midges and horse flies.

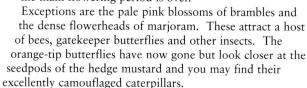

Keeled Skimmer

Warm evenings are good times to go out to hear and maybe see nightjars. This is one bird where camouflaging yourself is not necessary. The males are very inquisitive, being especially attracted by white objects. On one occasion I took my three month old son, Oscar, with me to look for them. He was strapped to my chest in a sling with his white socks sticking out. This attracted the male nightjar within seconds, circling us within a few feet before flying off to his churring post!

Nightjar

These strange birds visit us each year to make the most of a nocturnal food supply – moths. To go out 'mothing' with a lamp and a white sheet at this time of year can be amazing. The sheer variety and beauty of the moths attracted is quite staggering. Each one beautifully camouflaged for its daytime retreat.

For me certain scents and sounds are most evocative of high summer. Three in particular stand out: the sickly sweet smell of privet blossom on a warm evening as the heat radiates from the ground; the drawn out begging "pee-ooo" calls of young buzzards which echo around the hillsides; and the shimmering chorus of the great green bush-cricket at dusk after a hot day.

A trip to the coast is a refreshing way to escape the heat. If the tide is out there are few better ways of spending an afternoon than dabbling around in rockpools. The variety of plants and animals is incredible. Some are from such ancient lines

Montagu's Blenny

that at first it is difficult to tell if they are a plant or an animal.

Here the first signs of the approaching autumn can be seen. Shores and estuaries gradually fill with waders and gulls, whilst passage terns fish offshore as they gather reserves for their long journey south.

During the first week of August a sudden change takes place heralding the beginning of autumn – the swifts depart. One evening they are there screaming around the buildings as they have been all summer – then there is silence. This seems strange at first, especially on warm balmy evenings which seem perfect for them to be chasing around the rooftops. Though there are usually a few individuals to be found amongst the chattering house martins. Occasionally a large flock will appear towards the end of the month but their screaming calls will not be heard again until next spring.

Blackberries

Clear early mornings in late August have a distinct autumn chill about them. This vanishes with the dew by mid-morning as the grasshopper chorus starts up. These insects revel in the last of the summer's warmth. Berries appear and ripen in the hedgerows. By late August the blackberry harvest is in full swing for people and wildlife, and the first autumn robin song can be heard on cool mornings. This song, and the short chirrups of dark bush-crickets in the hedgebanks are sure signs that autumn has arrived.

Goldcrests courting. There is often a flourish of goldcrest activity in early June with a noticeable increase in song as they prepare to raise a second brood.

Whinchats – this pair had a nest containing three young concealed in a grass tussock. The female has just caught a small yellow spider.

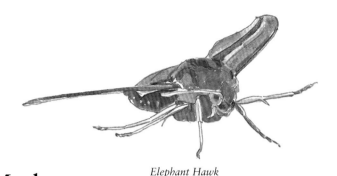

Elephant Hawk

Cloaked Carpet

Marbled Pug

Moths

To fully appreciate the beauty and sheer variety of these nocturnal insects it is necessary to go out at night with a light and a white sheet. Moths fly throughout the year with a peak in numbers and variety in July. Warm, humid summer nights, with a hint of thunder, are the best, when a staggering variety of species of all shapes and sizes may be drawn to the lamp.

Obviously, this varies with the habitat. Ancient woodlands are among the best. A visit to one on a good night can reveal amazing numbers of these nocturnal insects. Many have evocative names coined by Georgian entomologists. Carpets, gothics, arches, daggers and wainscots to name a few.

Bloxworth Snout

The flight times of the individual species is surprisingly ordered. Some flit around the hedges at dusk. Others fly just after dark and some do not make an appearance until after midnight. Hundreds of different species have been recorded in Devon and a few, including the Devon Carpet and Devonshire Wainscot have been named after the county where they were first discovered.

Visit the same area during the daytime and it is difficult to find more than a handful of specimens. Their often beautiful markings provide excellent camouflage against a wide variety of backgrounds.

Beautiful Golden Y

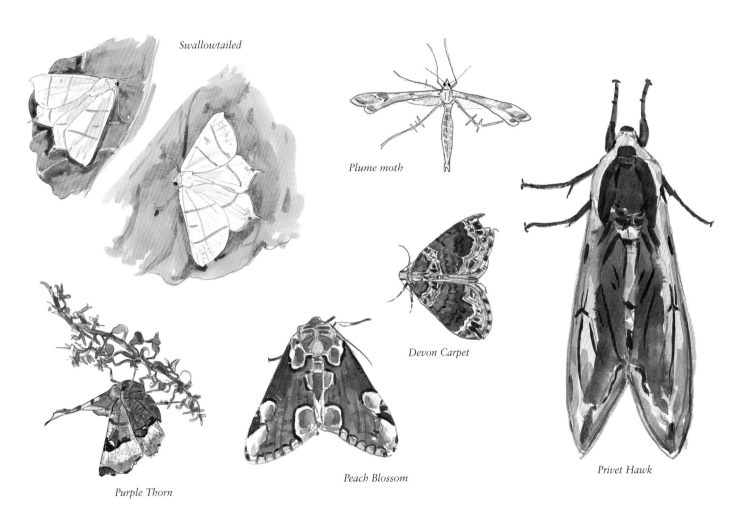

Swallowtailed

Plume moth

Devon Carpet

Privet Hawk

Purple Thorn

Peach Blossom

47

Great Spotted Woodpecker female feeding well grown young in nest. The nests of this species are usually very easy to find as the young call constantly. This nest was located at head height in an oak.

on Marsh St Johns Wort flowers
August 1999

cleaning tongue

Bog Hoverfly

This species has disappeared from much of its former range in southern England and Ireland. It can now only be found on Dartmoor where several strong colonies inhabit wet boggy areas which are grazed by cattle, sheep and ponies. The larvae have never been seen but are presumed to feed in the nutrient rich mud of these areas. The adults can be found throughout the summer often visiting bog flowers such as Bog-bean and Marsh St John's Wort.

Bog hoverflies (Eristalis cryptarum)

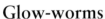

Glow worm larva

Glow-worms

There are few sights more magical than the pale glow of these insects on a midsummer night. In Devon they can be found in a variety of situations ranging from coastal grassland to woodland rides and hedgerows.

Glow-worms are in fact a species of beetle and only the female emits the light as an attraction to the flying males.

Their larvae feed on snails, which they suck dry. These unique insects take two years to develop, becoming fully grown in June.

female

male

Tanner beetle

This is one of the largest longhorn beetles to be found in this country. It is rare but may be found in a few localities in south Devon.

The adult beetles fly from late July to early September after spending several years as a larva feeding in the roots of trees.

I was incredibly lucky whilst cycling home one evening. I remembered that I had to pick some bramble leaves for a caterpillar I was keeping. As I was about to get back on my bike I noticed something crawling about in the grass between my feet. It was a male tanner beetle, running about surprisingly quickly for such a large insect.

I took it home to sketch. After dark it warmed itself up and whirred into action flying around the room in a fast but ungainly manner before it crash landed on the curtain! I released it the following day and have only seen a handful since.

downy
underside

Tanner Longhorn
Prionus coriarius ♂.
Bovey Great Plantation
crawled out from road
verge around my feet 5pm
27 August 1996
SX 814 755

sat quietly
on piece of bark

51

Great Green Bush-crickets

These impressive insects are the largest of the grasshoppers and bush-crickets found in this country. Being sun-loving, they are distinctly southerly in distribution, and most frequently found in coastal localities. Large colonies do exist inland, though in recent years these have become mainly confined to the south-west of England. Living close to one of these inland colonies is a real pleasure, especially on warm August evenings when the chorus of many hundreds of males calling together is a magical experience.

Late April or early May sees the appearance of the first nymphs, small green hoppers, amongst the fresh vegetation. Given warm conditions these feed up quickly, reaching maturity from late July with peak numbers of adults occuring in August. The nocturnal chorus of the males is at its best then, especially on warm, humid nights, when the air can be thick with their calls. In these conditions a typical daily pattern emerges. As the heat of the day wears off the first males call erratically in short bursts, as if warming up. Then, as dusk approaches, this builds gradually to an almost deafening peak just after dark. The full chorus lasts for an hour or so before gradually declining towards midnight.

'Crystal beads dropped in a stream down a crystal stair would produce a sound somewhat like the insect's song, but duller' was how W. H. Hudson beautifully described the song in his book *Hampshire Days*. It certainly has a delicate beauty about it, combining these crystal qualities with metallic shivering sounds similar to those made by rapidly rubbing two coins together.

Despite their size and loud calls they can be surprisingly difficult to find amongst the rough vegetation they inhabit. I have found that the easiest way to locate a calling male is to walk quickly towards the sound, stalling only when the insect itself pauses in its song. This often involves walking a surprising distance, but when you are getting close the call emitted by the insect seems to change subtly, taking on a different quality, as clicking sounds can be detected amongst the increased volume of the shivering notes.

When you are very close it is a matter of looking for the slight trembling movement of the wings that betrays the singer's location. The larger, mute females are often stumbled upon at this time. They quietly sit up on the vegetation often close to a calling male as they too listen to his song.

On cooler late summer and autumn days these large bush-crickets spend long periods sunning themselves on flat leaves, especially those of comfrey, dock and bramble. Here they can be observed at length as they lie flat against the surface to gain the maximum warmth of the sun. Now the chorus peaks during the late afternoon and can still be very impressive.

The sound level gradually declines during September before decreasing noticeably in the first weeks of October. The last males are usually heard in the third week of the month and thereafter only females can be found. These are usually to be seen sunning themselves on fine mornings and occasionally egg laying on warmer afternoons.

It is always sad to find the last dying individuals, often darkened in colour by the first frosts, as this really marks the end of another summer. But already I am looking forward to seeing the newly emerged nymphs next spring and anticipating the summer chorus of this magnificent insect.

♀ feeding on
♂ speckled
Bush-cricket

Allotment am
sunny quite
warm on slope

1 November 1998

Great green bush-crickets feed on leaves, blackberries and seeds as well as any insects that they can capture. They are keen hunters of smaller grasshoppers. Their amazingly long antennae and large goat-like eyes are used to detect their prey. This is held down with the spiny forelegs whilst the huge jaws make short work of their victim.

If these formidable predators are handled it must be done with great care, as their large jaws can easily cut through skin and draw blood!

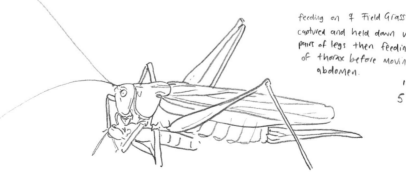

feeding on ♀ Field Grasshopper
captured and held down with front
pair of legs then feeding on base
of thorax before moving onto
abdomen.

in captivity
5 November 1998

The courtship of these bush-crickets is difficult to observe as it usually occurs out of sight in thick vegetation. The sole occasion I have witnessed it was on a warm afternoon in late September. I found a pair sunning themselves close together on a bramble leaf. The male was calling frantically, though the female didn't seem to be taking much notice. He would occasionally walk away from the leaf and call from a patch of nettles above her only to return a few minutes later. On one occasion the female moved up into the nettles with him and they mated. They remained together for over half an hour before the male moved off leaving the female suspended upside down on the nettle stem with the large spermatophore attached to the base of her abdomen.

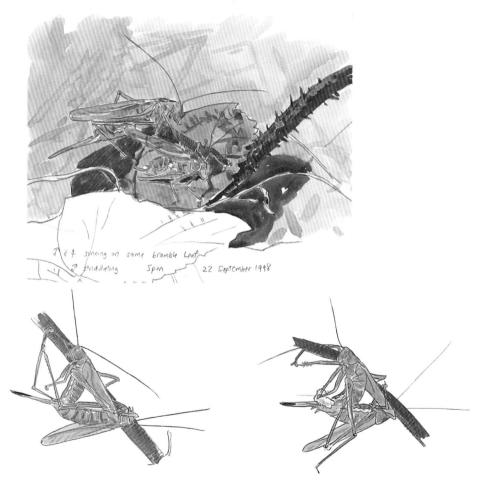

♂ & ♀ sunning on same bramble Leaf

♂ stridulating   5pm   22 September 1998

54

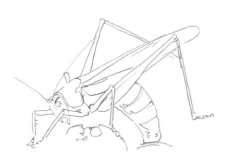

The egg laying female thrusts her long ovipositor deep into the soil.

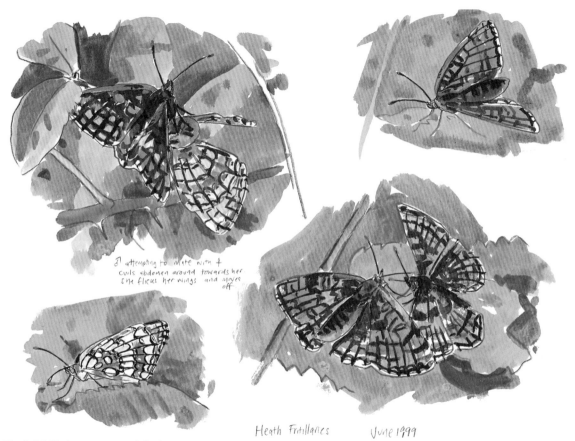

♂ attempting to mate with ♀
curls abdomen around towards her
she flicks her wings and moves
off

Heath Fritillaries   June 1999

Heath Fritillaries - once mated the females of this species bask in the sunshine for long periods before egg laying. They frequently have to ward off amorous males which attempt to mate with them. The male curls his abdomen towards the female, who reacts by flicking her wings rapidly until the male gets the message and moves on.

The larvae are superbly camouflaged on bracken.

High Brown Fritillary

Over the last forty years this species has declined more dramatically than any other British butterfly. This is probably due to changes in land management, especially a lack of woodland coppicing.

Fortunately the bracken slopes of Dartmoor provide an alternative habitat and it is one of the few remaining strongholds for this beautiful butterfly.

Here its life cycle is closely associated with bracken. The larvae, which hatch from overwintering eggs, feed on violets growing amongst bracken leaf litter. The sun warms the dead leaves providing a warm microclimate which the caterpillar requires. They can occasionally be found resting on dead bracken fronds, or feeding on violets during May.

The adults fly from late June to early August. By this time the bracken has reached its full height so the females have to fly down through holes in the canopy to lay their eggs near to violet plants.

The females descend to the ground below the bracken canopy to lay their eggs.

Young Swallows in the nest.

Swallow feeding newly fledged juvenile.

Swifts

The screaming of swifts on a warm, sunny evening is a wonderful sound. After feeding at high altitude during the day the birds gather over their colonies, which are usually in towns and cities, to feed, chase and preen. The strength of this evening activity is usually a reflection of the warmth of the day.

On cool, overcast evenings swifts are usually fairly quiet with just a few half-hearted chases, but after a hot day they are full of excitement. Chases are initiated by an individual raising its wings for a second, usually to just one other bird. Their calls then attract several more until a tight ball of screaming birds is formed. They race around the sky for a minute or so until the energy of the flock fades. This activity continues for an hour or so before dusk. Then most of the birds ascend to a great height in a tight group until they are lost to sight in the blue haze.

Summer thunderstorms present a major problem for these aerial birds. In these conditions they can be seen in large flocks flying along the edge of the storm cloud. The birds may fly hundreds of miles around the storm to avoid being grounded by heavy rain.

Swifts preening in flight.

60

swifts over town overcast but warm evening 15 July 1999 Buckfastleigh

Swifts and House Martins.

Jersey Tigermoth

This attractive day flying moth is found on the northern edge of its range in southern England. Although scattered colonies do occur along the south coast, the only place where it is really common is in south Devon. Here it occurs on rough ground, lanes and gardens from the coast up to the edge of Dartmoor.

The larvae which are not often seen feed on a variety of low-growing plants such as dock and dandelion. The adults fly from late July to early September and are often mistaken for butterflies. This also happens abroad. The famous 'valley of the butterflies' on Rhodes is actually an aestivation site for thousands of these moths.

Rockpools

Dabbling in rockpools is one of my favourite summer pastimes. The diversity of life amongst the beautiful weed filled pools can be amazing. It is incredible that anything can live in them at all. The extremes of summer heat, winter frosts, rain (diluting the pools) and winter storms makes the intertidal zone a seemingly inhospitable place to live.

At first glance there is little to see. Maybe a small fish darting into a crevice in a rockpool and layers of flattened seaweed. But look closer into the pools and search under the weed and stones and the life can be found.

Squat Lobster

Crabs, starfish, gobies, brittlestars, sea slugs – the list is endless. The sheer variety of life in the sea is mind boggling. Many of the animals are very primitive. Some, like the sea-squirts and sponges look more like plants but are actually groups of tiny creatures living together as one unit. Others are more spectacular. I vividly remember my first Velvet Swimming Crab. As I lifted a stone its red eyes stared back at me. It then lashed out with its blue spotted claws before scuttling off into the weed.

Cornish Clingfish

No two trips to the shore are the same. Amongst the regular anemones, crabs and fish there are always surprises. The best time to visit is at the time of a full or new moon. Then the spring tides reveal more of the shore than usual at low water. Squat lobsters can now be found along with some of the largest crabs to be seen on the shore.

Amongst the commoner Cornish Clingfish it is possible to find some closely related species – the tiny Small-headed Clingfish and the Montagu's Sea Snail. The Sea Snail hides under stones and on seaweed. I presume it is named from its habit of curling up in the shape of a snail's shell when at rest.

Montagu's Sea Snail

Montagu's Blenny

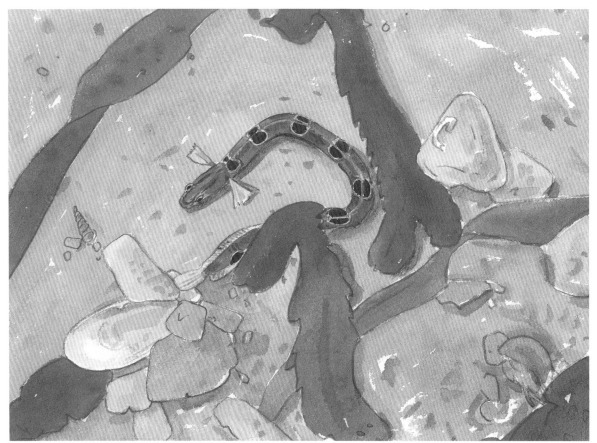

Butterfish – this eel like fish can be found sheltering under stones and seaweed at low tide. It has slippery skin making it very difficult to pick up.

Montagu's Blenny – a small fish which prefers to live in the pink encrusted rockpools high on the shore. This rare species was named after the naturalist George Montagu who discovered it in south Devon during the early part of the 19th century.

Masked Crab Goodrington Paignton
5 April 1999
Found walking on sand near low tide mark - quickly buried itself
in sand when I put it into a small pool - leaving just its periscope
nose visible.

Masked crabs usually remain hidden under the sand during the day. This one was found on the surface near the low tide mark and was lucky not to have been picked off by a herring gull.

I released it into a small pool. Within seconds it had disappeared, with just its snorkel nose visible above the sand.

mating pair

produces purple pink
dye if disturbed

Sea Hares in the pink corraline seaweed pools of the upper shore. These slugs move inshore to breed during the spring and early summer. They can produce a purple ink if disturbed.

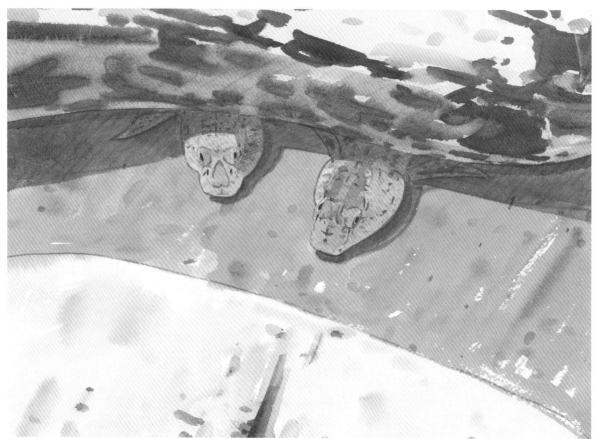

Giant Gobies - these fish can only be found along the south coasts of Devon and Cornwall in this country. They grow up to 27cm long and live in bare, brackish rockpools high on the shore. Like most rockpool fish gobies can change their skin colour to match the surrounding rocks. They are usually easy to observe if approached carefully.

Velvet Swimming Crabs   January 2000

Velvet Swimming Crabs - these crabs are usually common on rocky beaches. Also known as the 'Devil Crab'
because of their red eyes and fiery temperament.

Wood Ants

Wood ants are remarkable insects. In the woods on the southern slopes of Dartmoor they are especially common. Stand on a still summer day in one of these woods and an audible rustle can be heard amongst the dry leaves. The noise comes from thousands of these industrious insects busying themselves collecting food and nest material.

Their nests are often large domes made up of twigs and leaves or pine needles, depending on the locality. Nests are often interconnected by an 'ant motorway' up to ten metres long.

The ants get everywhere, climbing trees as well as scouring the ground and bringing home a surprising range of prey from caterpillars to beetles and flies. It seems amazing that any other insects can survive alongside them.

Their strength, stamina and teamwork are what really impress me. At one nest which I frequently watch they have to carry their bounty up a vertical bank, which is about half a metre high. Often it takes them several attempts to ascend. One ant struggling with a twig is often joined by others. They may pull in opposite directions for a while but then gradually move the huge object up to the nest. The equivalent of two people carrying a large tree trunk up a sheer cliff face!

A wood ants nest would seem an inhospitable place for any small insects to make a home, but remarkably many species of beetles inhabit them.

The Scarce Seven-spot Ladybird can occasionally be found around the ant nests. They are virtually ignored by the ants and move about at leisure. The ants probably provide them with some protection from other invertebrate predators whilst the ladybirds feed on the aphids which the wood ants tend for honeydew.

Wood Ants carrying nest
material – amazing strength –
if one ant gets swung up
mid air at the other end of
the stick
Bilberryhill 25 July 1999

Marbled Whites

These distinctive butterflies occur in grasslands ranging from those along the coast to the rhôs pastures of Dartmoor. They are colonial and often locally abundant.

On sunny days they fly actively amongst the grasses, pausing occasionally to nectar on knapweed and bramble flowers.

At dusk, after a hot day, it is worth visiting a colony to observe their roosting behaviour. Being conspicuous insects marbled whites attempt to conceal themselves by resting on or near to white flowers. In a small colony near my home it is possible to see over forty individuals roosting on yarrow heads.

Being limited for time in the evening I painted these in the early morning light before the dew had dried from the grasses and the snails had retired for the day.

Marbled Whites

G Spei Burnett
Marbled whites
Meadow Grasshoppers

Deptford Pink
Church Hill Buckfastleigh
100s of plants flowering behind
industrial estate
4 July 1999

Deptford Pink - this plant has declined dramatically over the last fifty years. It is usually found growing in disturbed ground, often beside tracks and paths. As its name suggests it was once widespread in London. Old sites include Tottenham Court Road, where any suitable habitat has long disappeared under tarmac. Why it has declined in other parts of the country is still a mystery. I only know of one site where it is common. Here it grows in the thin soil of a south facing road cutting and thrives as there are few other plants to compete with.

Six-spot Burnet

11 am   9 August 1998
Mardle Way
Industrial Estate

warm sunny

The sunny slope where I drew the Marbled White butterflies and Deptford Pink is also home to some day flying moths. As burnet moths are distasteful to most birds they sit around openly on flowerheads displaying their warning colours.

The Six-belted Clearwing closely resembles a small wasp – though it is completely harmless. Its larvae feed on the roots of Birds-foot Trefoil. The best way to find the adult moths is to search on dead flowerheads where they can be found at rest.

On one occasion I watched one being attacked by a wasp. The moth's reactions were amazingly quick. It fell like a stone into the grass below and remained motionless for a minute or so. Meanwhile the wasp, not locating any movement moved on.

Six-belted Clearwing

Autumn

Autumn is a time of gradual slowing down and taking stock in the countryside. Through September the long daylight hours and heat of summer fade, to be replaced by shorter evenings and more changeable weather. Although a period of gradual closing down in the countryside it is still a beautiful time of year. A clear blue morning has a precious beauty about it after a period of westerly gales and heavy rain. On these days the afternoon sunshine is still warm instilling a relaxed atmosphere in the countryside.

The summer migrant birds are steadily departing. The swallows and martins are amongst the most noticeable as they gather in large flocks. House martin numbers remain high until the autumn solstice and then rapidly dwindle. They often gather on rooftops to make the most of the morning sunshine. Some still have young in the nest at this time of year, the broods being tended by the young of earlier broods as well as the adult pair. The same situation occurs in moorhens which can often be seen with their new broods on dykes and ponds well into the autumn.

House Martin

Amongst thickets of elder and blackberry the furtive shapes of warblers can be seen. Stand still by the bush and the migrant blackcaps and garden warblers can be watched as they gorge themselves before their long migrations.

Most insects have put in an appearance by late summer with a few exceptions. The brown hairstreak is the latest of all the resident butterflies to emerge. It may be glimpsed in tree-lined blackthorn hedges from late August through September. Other insects are more noticeable at this time of year, especially wasps and hornets, as their numbers build to a peak. A strange fly which mimics them can also be seen at this time of year. The hornet robberfly can be found in open meadows sitting at its sentry post waiting to ambush passing insects.

Reptiles become more visible again as they have to spend longer periods of time warming up each day. Adders and common lizard can be very approachable as they warm their bodies for the last few times before retiring to their hibernation sites.

Freshly ploughed fields can attract gatherings of buzzards. These can number over fifty birds enticed by a rich picking of earthworms and beetles.

As the oaks shed their acorns a great race to store this valuable larder begins. Jays can be seen making short flights with full crops as they prepare their winter larders in competition with grey squirrels.

The first frosts usually occur in October. On crisp, clear mornings the sharp calls of goldcrests and long-tailed tits become more prominent in the hedgerows.

Shaggy Ink Caps

October days can swing from summer to winter depending on the weather. A sunny day can be as warm as any in September with a last buzz of insects around the ivy bloom. The next could be overcast with a dull dampness more typical of mid-winter. In these mild damp conditions fungi abound in woodlands and meadows in an amazing variety of shapes and sizes.

Along the riverbanks grey wagtails pick their way amongst the trickle of autumn leaves. They and the dippers are now revitalised as they set up their winter territories on the newly swollen rivers. On the last warm days large rafts of pond skaters can be seen on quiet backwaters along the edges of rivers, feeding up before hibernation.

River Pond Skaters

As sallow catkins provided the first feast of the year, the last is provided by ivy bloom. On sunny days an incredible mass of insects converge on any good patches which in turn attract the attention of birds. Amongst the mass of flies are usually a few stunning red admirals, at their best in the bright clear autumn light amongst the dark shadows of the ivy.

Orb Spider

Autumn spiders webs are everywhere, catching the dew on clear mornings. Orb spiders are the most noticeable species but in a few localities the spectacular wasp spider can be found. These are fully fattened females which will soon lay their eggs and die.

There is a final flush of colour in November as the leaves turn to yellow and orange standing brilliantly in the dull damp weather typical of this time of year. The sunshine has now become weak, only in a few sheltered spots is any warmth created and then only during the middle of the day. The last dark bush-crickets call in the hedgerows, red admirals can still be active and even a few dragonflies can be seen but the year is almost over for these warmth loving creatures.

Newly arrived redwings and fieldfares spread over the countryside gathering where the berry harvest is greatest and a few blackcaps skulk in the orchards. These birds will spend the winter with us feeding on windfall apples and later in gardens.

Long-tailed tit flocks are obvious in the hedgerows often joined by other tits and goldcrests. The noisy parties make their way along the lanes pausing for a while amongst some late sycamore leaves in a sheltered spot. Finally a stormy day blows the last of the leaves away. Then a cold snap in November cleans away any last traces of summer and settles the countryside into a pattern of winter activity.

Brown Hairstreak – this is an extremely elusive butterfly. It spends most of the time sitting around high in tall hedges and oak trees.

I found this one almost by accident whilst picking some sloes on a bright September morning.

The eggs are much easier to find than the adult butterflies! They are white and usually situated at the base of a thorn.

1·10pm
Church Hill
Buckfastleigh

picking some
sloes at the top
of the hill - keeping
a look out for Brown
Hairstreaks - suddenly
one was there sitting
on a tip of Blackthorn
a large
hairstreak.
quite sluggish
sitting around
on bushes flying
occasionally.

7 September 1996

some specimens with huge fat bodies ready to lay eggs

remains of previous meal left in web

egg sac suspended above ground amongst dead grass stems
west Hayling Shore
1 September 1996

life size

stripled + legs

Wasp Spider (Argiope bruennichi)
This striking spider has become
established in south Devon during the
last decade. It is mainly found in
coastal grasslands. The males are
smaller and less conspicuous than the
females. These are usually seen on
their webs low in the grasses where
they prey on grasshoppers.

The large egg sac is the winter home
for the young spiderlings. They hatch
during the autumn but wait for a
warm spring day before venturing out.

Moorhens   Safeways Totnes   21 August 1999

*Moorhen with young. These birds nest in a dyke close to Safeways Supermarket in Totnes. Having a ready
supply of food, thrown to them by passing people, they are able to raise three broods during a season.*

Moorhen with young.

Teign Estuary

Estuaries are great places for birdwatching. Find the right place to sit and the birds will come to you. All these drawings and paintings were made in the same place at the head of the estuary near the Passage House Inn. I would usually arrive about two and a half hours before high tide. At this time the water's edge would be way in the distance but being a flat estuary the tide rushes in at a rate of knots. No two tides are the same, the pattern of birds is always subtly different. Sometimes the curlews crowd on the last saltmarsh island before flying off to roost, on other occasions a group of little egrets gather there and on another it is cormorants with an accompanying grey heron. These surprise combinations of birds draw me back again and again.

Gulls and carrion crows dominate the scene here. The crows are expert crab catchers and can often be seen holding their prey down with one foot and dismembering the victim with their beak.

As the tide pushes the birds closer the line of gulls, crows, egrets and waders come closer. I have to sketch and paint rapidly knowing that the tide will soon displace me from the saltmarsh.

Whilst concentrating on painting I have frequently been caught out by the tide as it breaches the saltmarsh and rushes in leaving me to rescue my floating paint pots and escape to dry land! On these big spring tides other creatures are caught out as well. Wading back I have occasionally seen shrews, which had ventured out to feed amongst the saltmarsh grasses, swimming frantically alongside me to reach dry land.

Grey Heron about to bathe.

82

Foot-paddling Black-headed Gulls.

Black-headed Gulls and Carrion Crow.

Curlews, Black-headed Gulls and a Little Egret roosting as the tide advances.

Teign Estuary Passage House Inn 1 September 1993 sunny calm warm

Black-headed Gulls, Carrion Crows and a traffic cone washed down by the river.

Roosting Little Egret and Redshanks facing a strong wind.

The Buzzard field

Cycling home on a sunny evening in September 1995, I noticed some buzzards in a field adjacent to a busy main road. Within yards of the commuter traffic a group of up to twenty individuals ran, bounced and flew around after earthworms and beetles. Two or three times a week throughout October I set up my telescope at the edge of this field and sketched and painted the birds. The thundering of the rush hour traffic faded into the distance as I became engrossed in the antics of the feeding birds. By late October I had made many sketches and paintings of them and was surprised how tolerant they were of each other. Although there were many occasions when two individuals would home in on the same worm they rarely showed any aggression.

A few individuals remained into November and one, in particular, would often fly up from the roadside as I passed at dusk. During a cold spell in January I found this bird lying dead at the entrance to the field. I took it home to sketch and photograph and it remained outside our back door for a few days proving to be of some interest to the local cats and the postman!

October 1995. Oak road. Alston Cross. A31. sunny mild. 10.15 am. 12 buzzards in field. JMW

Buzzards hunting earthworms.

Alsager Cross 1 November 1995

A dramatic pounce on an earthworm!

Grey Wagtail, River Mardle, Church Street, Buckfastleigh, sunny, 25 October 1999

Grey wagtail amongst autumn leaves.

House Martins Chapel Street Buckfastleigh late brood leaving nest   10 September 1999

Late broods of house martins leave the nest during September. The young are fed by the parents and young birds from earlier broods.

On a sunny October morning ivy blossom attracts many insects – the Red Admirals are at their best in the bright autumn sunlight against the dark foliage.

Greenshanks

A loud 'tu-tu-tu" is usually the first indication of the
presence of these birds on a coastal estuary. They breed in
the far north of Scotland, Iceland and the Arctic, prefering
wild expanses of tundra in which to raise their young.
After the brief northern summer they move south to their
wintering grounds. August is the peak month for them on
the south coast of England. At this time small parties can
be observed around the coast of Devon, especially on the
Exe Estuary.

Larger and more distinguished looking than the redshank,
the greenshanks stand out in the crowd with their clean
white underparts and long pale green legs.

To sketch these birds I like to arrive at a particular spot on
the estuary at high tide to observe the roosting birds.
Usually several can be found loafing around, idly preening
or sleeping amongst the redshanks. As the tide ebbs they
move out onto the newly exposed mudflats in ones and
twos. I make a move too and set up my telescope tucked in
under the seawall.

At this state of the tide these birds are at their best. They
like to feed on small fish in the shallow water as the tide
recedes. They chase around wildly, bill tips in the water
ready to strike. They often work in pairs or even larger
groups and twist and turn with amazing agility as they
chase the fry.

Greenshanks chasing fish fry as the tide ebbs.

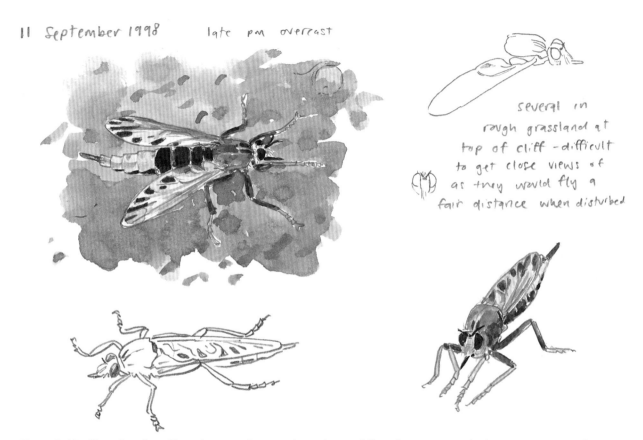

11 September 1998   late pm overcast

several in rough grassland at top of cliff – difficult to get close views of as they would fly a fair distance when disturbed

Hornet Robberflies – these large flies wait on prominent perches such as ant hills and cow pats to ambush passing insects. Little is know about their life cycle. Though it is thought that their larvae feed underground and prey on the larvae of dung beetles.

Hornets

Although fearsome in appearance, hornets are much more docile than their cousin the common wasp. I found this nest in a hollow of an ancient beech tree on the edge of an oakwood. It was located at about head height allowing me to watch their activities at close range.

They only became agitated if I moved too close to the nest. Then one of the guards would sound the alarm calling out the rest of the colony. The hornets then sat on the nest fanning their wings.

One individual eventually chased me off. It seemed to use its size and loud buzz as a deterrent rather than trying to sting me. I got the message and beat a hasty retreat!

Hornets guarding nest in old beech tree Potato Field Newbridge 19 October 1999

Fairy Shrimps

These small creatures can only survive in a most unusual habitat – temporary pools which dry out at least once each year. Permanent pools attract larger predators such as dragonfly nymphs which would feed on the defenceless shrimps.

Because of the very nature of their habitat they have a rapid life cycle. Their eggs lie dormant in the mud until a period of heavy rain fills the pool, then the tiny shrimps hatch and have a race against time before the pool dries up again. During the summer months any that hatch often do not make it – they can be found crowded into the last puddles of water as the sun dries the mud to dust.

During the spring and autumn conditions are usually more suitable and a visit to the pools a couple of weeks after heavy rain will find the pool full of full grown shrimps. They are fairly large (four centimetres long) and swim on their backs propelling themselves along with their constantly moving legs.

They are translucent and easier to detect in sunny weather by looking for their shadows. They share the environment with waterfleas, bloodworms and a variety of small water beetles.

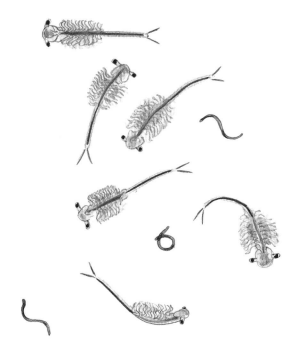

Fairy Shrimps and bloodworms.

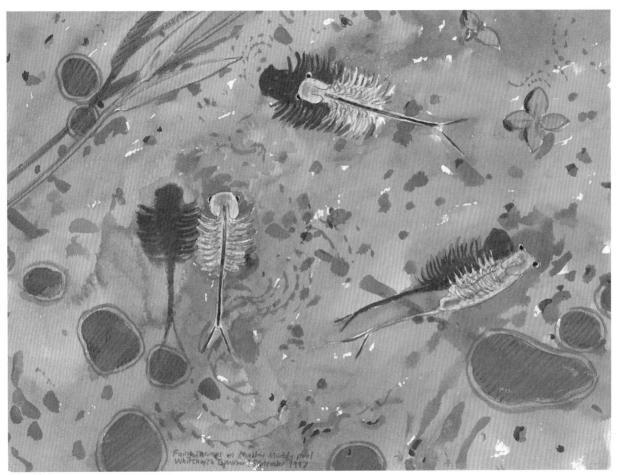

Fairy Shrimps

Grey Squirrels

Although not always the most popular of animals, grey squirrels have now become a familiar sight in the Devon countryside. The native red squirrels, once widespread in the area, were last seen in the 1970s.

Autumn is a time of great activity in the squirrel population, as they prepare for winter. Early autumn sees them stripping the unripe hazelnuts from the hedges. If it has been a good year for acorns they spend most of October days collecting the nuts and burying them. Often there will be several squirrels around one tree along with the local jays who also use the acorn crop as a winter larder.

Rather than taking the acorns far to hide them, most squirrels seem to bury them in the roots of grasses and then disguise the hiding place by brushing dead leaves over it with their forepaws.

They also hoard sweet chestnuts if they are available, carefully prising the nuts from their green spiky cases.

Grey Squirrel hiding an acorn in a grass tussock, then covering the hiding place with some leaves.

Grey squirrels collecting acorns.

Grey squirrel collecting sweet chestnuts.

swallowed 5 or 6 acorns
before flying off and hiding
them in grass tussocks.

Jays Parke December 1994

*I have always found Jays to be extremely wary birds which are difficult to approach. To sketch these I
collected a bag full of acorns during the autumn. Then in December I placed them on tree trunks and on the
ground under a large oak. The local Jays soon found them. By using a telescope I could get excellent views
as they collected the acorns and hid them in nearby grass tussocks.*

*After hiding an acorn in a grass tussock Jays often
cover the site with an oak leaf.*

Winter

In contrast to the activity of the autumn, early winter is a quiet time of year. The hours of daylight steadily decrease and the weather is often mild and damp. There are some new arrivals. Most noticeable are the redwings and fieldfares. The thin "seep" calls of redwings are a familar sound on clear nights in November.

The harsh "chacking" calls of fieldfares are more often heard in remote areas like Dartmoor. Here they feast on hawthorn berries in the hedges. These winter thrushes are wary birds. It takes a period of icy weather to bring them out of the fields to find food in gardens.

String-of-Sausages or Beard Lichen

During the winter gardens become excellent places to watch birds. My own, which is situated in a town on the edge of Dartmoor, regularly attracts siskins, greenfinches, and blue tits to the feeders. These are joined by ground feeders such as dunnocks, robins and blackbirds. Occasional sightings of meadow pipits and black redstarts on the lawn and blackcaps in the honeysuckle are welcome surprises.

Black Redstart

As gales and frost finally strip the hedgerows of their leaves during December, a host of ferns and lichens are uncovered. Most obvious of these are the hartstongue ferns, but a closer look reveals other species such as the polypody and black spleenwort. Lichens are good indicators of the prevailing clean Atlantic air which blows over south-west England. Dartmoor is a particularly good area for one species, the spectacular, string-of-sausages or beard lichen. This can be seen hanging in swathes from the branches at a small number of locations.

Few birds inhabit the high moorland areas during the winter. The conditions here are much harsher than in the lowlands, with a far higher chance of snow. Golden plovers seem to prefer the bleakest areas where they can feed undisturbed. Amongst the smaller birds a few stonechats, skylarks and meadow pipits remain on the open moor. The latter are the favourite prey of wintering merlins. Another bird of prey which can now be seen is the hen harrier. It is well worth braving the elements to see a beautiful pale grey male quartering over the dark heather to flush out its prey.

Many creatures can be found hibernating if you know where to look. The orange-tip caterpillars of summer overwinter as pupae. These are superbly camouflaged amongst dead stems in the hedgerow.

Orange-tip pupa

Hibernating queen wasp

Palmate newts can be found under stones, sometimes several will be found intertwined. Queen wasps and hornets can be found hibernating. They make a cell under dead bark and sit tight with their delicate wings folded under their abdomen.

Estuaries and coastal marshes are exciting places to visit at this time of year. Waders, wildfowl and gulls gather in huge numbers at these sites to overwinter. A wide variety of wildfowl are present including mallard, teal, wigeon and brent geese. Most elegant of the waders is the avocet. These can be seen in large flocks, especially on the Exe and Tamar.

By new year winter patterns of activity are firmly established. Long-tailed tit flocks are frequently seen in the hedgerows, often accompanied by other tits and goldcrests. These tiny birds need to be constantly active in search of food if they are to survive the winter. A prolonged spell of icy weather can be disastrous for them.

If cold weather persists many birds from mainland Europe arrive to seek shelter in the mild climate of south west England. Snow cover will result in large flocks of lapwings gathering on coastal marshes. Numbers of the winter thrushes and skylarks can increase dramatically in a few days.

Mallard

Other species such as the usually nocturnal woodcock and snipe, are forced to feed by day and become much easier to see.

Even in mid-winter signs of the approaching spring can be found. In this, one of the mildest parts of the country, spring comes early. Fresh honeysuckle leaves first appear before christmas, though any further growth is often halted by brief periods of frosty weather. These rarely last long though and by early February the gloom of mid-winter lifts for the first time around midday. The song of the mistle thrush grows stronger and on sunny days there is a real feel of spring.

Raven

One of the earliest breeding birds is the raven. During late winter they are at their most active. Low "gronk" calls fill the air close to their traditional nesting sites. Their spectacular aerial displays are a prelude to courtship and mating. In south Devon they are often on eggs by the end of February. As their chicks hatch and grow the weather becomes warmer and winter patterns of activity fade away. The winter thrushes are still present in large numbers at the beginning of March. But by the end of the month they have gone for another year and the hedgerow flowers are bursting from the bare earth banks.

The first warm days mark the end of winter. Now their is a real feel of anticipation in the air as another spring and summer of activity unfolds in the Devon countryside.

Mandarins Parke 18 October 1995 10.6.8.4 pm pair started to display then joined by rest – eventually all returned to bank and walked off in a line through the bankside trees.

Mandarin Ducks – this introduced species from the Far East has become well established in southern England. Around the southern fringes of Dartmoor they favour small tree-fringed rivers and ponds. As I sat watching this flock of ten birds they all swam out onto a small pond and the males began to display.

Snipe forced to feed during the day in a period of icy weather.

Redwings and fieldfares feeding together during cold weather.

Green Woodpecker with Redwing flock.

Meadow Pipits

I have a special affection for the meadow pipit. In my early birdwatching days small flocks arriving from the sea on the Hampshire coast were always a welcome sign of spring.
I especially enjoy watching and listening to their simple display flight and trilling song over the heaths and moors they inhabit. It is one of the commonest breeding birds on Dartmoor. Most move south to winter in France, Spain and North Africa, whilst a few remain to brave the winter in this country. These usually inhabit the lowland countryside and the coast.

It was a flock of these wintering birds that I first noticed on my bike ride home in September 1991. They were easy to observe as they gathered prior to roosting in the late afternoon. They spent their time preening on some wires which crossed a small area of heathland. The roost built up during October and by the end of that month I began to sketch them. The thick heather and western gorse on the heath provides comfort and safety for the roosting birds and draws in pipits from miles around. Their regular routine of gathering up on the wires to preen before dropping into the heather to roost coincided with my own bike ride home. This provided me with many opportunities to sketch them.

Throughout November I kept visiting the site adding to my collection of sketches. Being limited for time, the sketching had to be fast and intensive. Most of the poses I was trying to capture on paper would only last for a second or so. So I would try and freeze each in my mind and get it down on paper as fast as possible.

With the shorter days of December the birds were often on the wires for only a few minutes. Now they had to use every available minute of daylight to search for food. But by February, with the lighter evenings and milder weather, they had more time to idle and spent longer periods on the wires. Clear, calm evenings were best though windy and wet conditions gave some interesting poses not seen at other times.

By March the numbers had started to dwindle. On the first warm day which brought out the tortoiseshell and brimstone butterflies the pipits started displaying. Being birds of open country they would usually fly to some height above the heath to advertise their territory. Here they often sang from the wires which provide an elevated perch. As this display commenced the winter flock dispersed rapidly. Whether these had been winterers from northern areas or local birds was impossible to say.

Over the next few winters I continued observing and sketching them. By checking my previous year's notebook I could time my arrival to coincide with the pipits first appearance on the wires each evening.

Meadow pipits are very neat and tidy birds and spend a lot of time preening. Head scratching is always interesting to observe as the bird balances on one leg whilst bringing the other over the wing to scratch its head rapidly. The action would usually last a couple of seconds, which called for some rapid sketching. Repeat observation was the key to working out exactly what was happening and capturing the movement on paper.

I had read of another roost, in heather, on the edge of the moor. So, one January afternoon, I visited this site and found the birds using a small birch tree to sit and preen in.

The weather would often change considerably in the short but steep climb onto the moor. I often found myself in low cloud. My first painting of them there was in murky, damp weather. The drizzle had the effect of softening the watercolour paint and enhancing the picture. This gave it the undeniable hallmark of a field painting.

One evening the individual I was sketching suddenly froze then stretched out lengthways along the branch it was sitting on. As I looked up to see what the danger was a male hen harrier stalled just a few feet away. He looked as shocked as myself and lacked any of this species' usual grace as he flapped off hurriedly towards the open moor.

Over nine winters I have spent countless hours watching these birds and have amassed a huge file of sketches and paintings. Especially during the first weeks I spent sketching them I think I learnt more about drawing than I had ever done before. Concentrating on the same subject for many hours opened my eyes and changed forever the way in which I observed wildlife subjects.

I now appreciated that to really get to know any particular species requires a huge amount of intense observation. Even then you find that you are just scratching the surface. Rather than becoming tired of watching the same birds for many hours, I began to truly observe and record the subjects with a new depth of vision. From this understanding any species now has the potential to become a lifetimes work.

Even after all those hours I always stop to watch any pipits I see. I simply never tire of watching their simple but beautiful display flights on spring and summer days and take the opportunity to draw them whenever possible.

Meadow pipits at dusk in light drizzle.

100+ Meadow Pipits on wires Knighton Heath 4:45pm clear calm 15 January 1998

Meadow Pipits at pre-roost gathering on telegraph wires.

Meadow Pipits preening on wires.

The 'Pipit tree'.

Greenfinches are regular visitors to gardens where they enjoy peanuts and sunflower seeds. In the hedgerows they can often be seen feeding on rosehips.

Greenfinches feeding on rosehips
Dartington Cider Press 10 December 1999

Bullfinches – sketching these birds is never easy due to their timid nature. Late winter is always the best time to observe them as they feed on buds and seeds in the bare hedgerows. These were feeding on buddleia seeds in a walled garden. They were puffed out against the cold as they fed on a January morning.

Magpie roost

Central Park in Plymouth has one of the largest magpie roosts in the country. Up to 300 birds have been observed roosting in a line of horse chestnut trees close to Plymouth Argyle's football ground. Although city centres aren't always my first choice of places to sketch wildlife a trip can be a convenient way to combine shopping and sketching.

On my first visit I was surprised just how close to the football ground the birds were. Sketching birds with the roar of a football crowd only yards away was certainly a new experience for me. I stayed until the light faded as over 200 magpies gradually assembled in the row of trees that evening.

Whilst sketching at the the roost one damp, misty November afternoon I observed some of the birds holding their wings out, at their sides. They seemed to be enjoying the drizzle and taking an opportunity to have a wash.

Plymouth Argyle were at home that afternoon and an early goal set the crowd alight and sent the magpies scattering in all directions, chattering excitedly. They returned slowly after a few minutes and were not so bothered when Argyle put in a second!

Magpies in the roost on a windy February afternoon.

118

Magpies in the roost. One of the birds is feeding on a horse chestnut bud.

119

Cirl Buntings &
Yellowhammer
Ag Nose Prawle   14 November 1999

South Devon is now the only place in this country where Cirl Buntings still breed regularly. They are increasing in numbers thanks to some effective habitat management. This includes leaving stubble fields for them to feed in during the winter. Here a pair are sitting with their commoner relative – a male Yellowhammer.

Cirl Buntings Prawle
14 November 1999

cold E wind
mainly overcast

Cirl Buntings

Blackcaps

These warblers have become an increasingly common sight during the winter in this country. The mild climate of Devon seems to be particularly suitable for them to overwinter. Late in the autumn blackcaps are usually to be found in old orchards feeding on the last of the apple crop. From November onwards they are more frequently found in gardens feeding on berries, those of the honeysuckle being a favourite. I have also seen them feeding on bread and other scraps.

During the late winter blackcaps can still be found in gardens but tend to congregate around good patches of ivy where they feed avidly on the ripening berries. The males start singing on sunny days from mid-February onwards. Most of these garden visitors move on during March whilst newly arrived birds settle in scrub and woodland to breed.

Female blackcap swallowing a cotoneaster berry.

122

Blackcaps in honeysuckle.

123

Waxwings usually spend the winter in Scandinavia. Occasionally when the berry crop fails there they move further afield to find food. They are usually seen on the North Sea coast but occasionally a few wander as far as south-west England. I found this one by accident. My computer mouse had broken on New Year's Eve, so a shopping expedition into Plymouth was called for. Amongst the hoardes of sales shoppers I found this Waxwing feeding on some Rowan trees right in front of a McDonald's Restaurant. Not the most scenic of sites but a nice surprise!

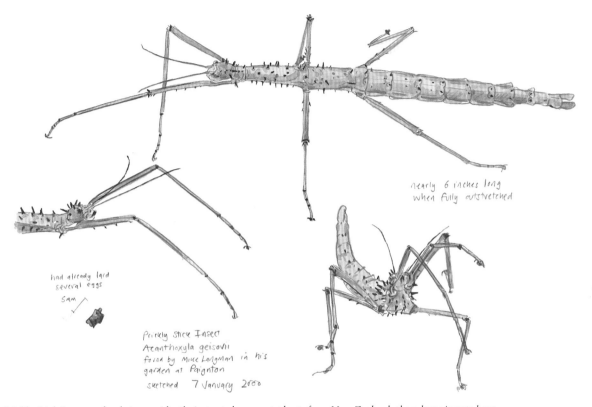

nearly 6 inches long
when fully outstretched

had already laid
several eggs

5mm

Prickly Stick Insect
Acanthoxyla geisovii
found by Mike Langman in his
garden at Paignton
sketched 7 January 2000

Prickly Stick Insect - after being accidently imported amongst plants from New Zealand, these large insects have now become established in the mildest areas of south west England. In Devon they have been found in small colonies around Torbay since 1907. They are usually found in gardens feeding on cypress bushes and Japanese larch - providing quite a surprise for local residents! Males of this species are unknown as the females are parthonogenic, each being able to produce hundreds of fertile eggs. They usually die off by late autumn but this individual was found in a particularly sheltered garden in early January.

Coots - these belligerent birds are always quick to pick a fight.

Countess Wear, Exeter – 3 December 1995

Cormorants at Countess Wear, Exeter. These large birds look a little incongruous perched up on wires and pylons.
But as they often perch on dead branches it is no surprise that they have adopted these 'metal trees' for their roost site.

Avocets – flocks of these graceful waders spend the winter on the sheltered estuaries of south-west England. The Exe Estuary is a particularly good site for them. On a winter's afternoon a few hundred can be seen on the mudflats at low tide. They move about in small parties sifting the mud with a sideways action of their heads. At high tide they do not usually head for dry land as other waders do, but sit swimming in small flocks in the middle of the estuary.

Goldfinches on teasels.

129

Ravens carrying nest material.

Raven pair chasing Jackdaws near nest site. Bullycleaves Quarry. 26 February 2000

Ravens chasing Jackdaws around their nest site in a quarry.

The explosive song of a male Cetti's Warbler is usually the first indication of the presence of this bird. It braves the winter in this country and can only survive in mild areas along the south coast.

Slapton Ley is a particuarly good place for them. Even here, where they are fairly common, they are difficult to see. A typical sighting is of a small brown bird flying low between clumps of reeds.

On this occasion two birds were chasing each other around. Then they flew across the road to a garden. Here they could be watched out in the open as they flitted around the branches next to a male House Sparrow.

two Cetti's Warblers (pair?) singing, in reeds then flew across read into gardens in bush with House Sparrow.

Torcross, Slapton Ley 11 February 1996 pm

132